DATE DUE

D1418015

DEMCO

For every cup and plateful,
Lord, make us truly grateful.

A CHILD'S BOOK OF GRACES
Copyright © 2006 by Good Books,
Intercourse, PA 17534
International Standard Book Number:
1-56148-514-4
Library of Congress Catalog Card Number:
2005025132

Written and compiled by Lois Rock
All unattributed prayers by Lois Rock
Illustrations copyright © 2005 Alison Jay

Original edition published in English under
the title *A Child's Book of Graces* by
Lion Hudson, plc, Oxford, England.
Copyright © Lion Hudson 2005.

North American edition entitled **A Child's Book
of Graces** published by Good Books, 2006.

Printed and bound in Singapore.

Library of Congress Cataloging-in-
Publication Data

Rock, Lois, 1953-
   A child's book of graces /
written and compiled by Lois Rock ;
illustrations, Alison Jay.
      p. cm.
   ISBN 1-56148-514-4 (hardcover)
   1. Grace at meals--Juvenile literature.
I. Jay, Alison. II. Title.
   BV283.G7R63 2006
   242'.82--dc22

                              2005025132

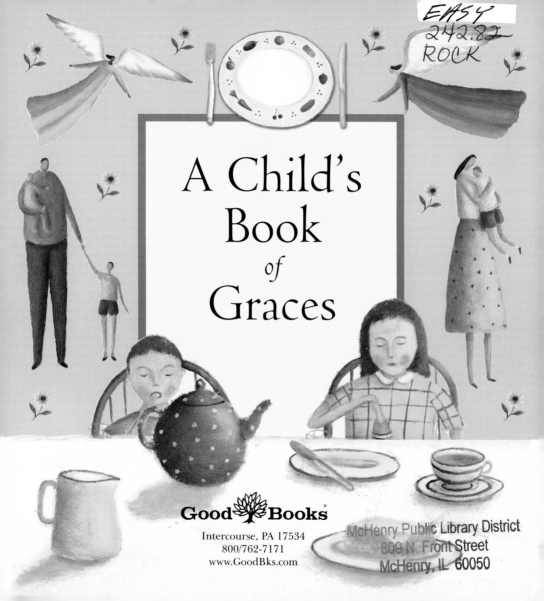

A Child's Book of Graces

Good Books

Intercourse, PA 17534
800/762-7171
www.GoodBks.com

In the morning

Morning is here,
The table is spread,
Thanks be to God,
Who gives us bread.

Anonymous

For health and strength
and daily food,
we praise your name,
O Lord.

Traditional

Alone and quietly

Dear God,
I gratefully bow my head
To thank you for my daily bread,
And may there be a goodly share
On every table everywhere. Amen.

A Mennonite children's prayer

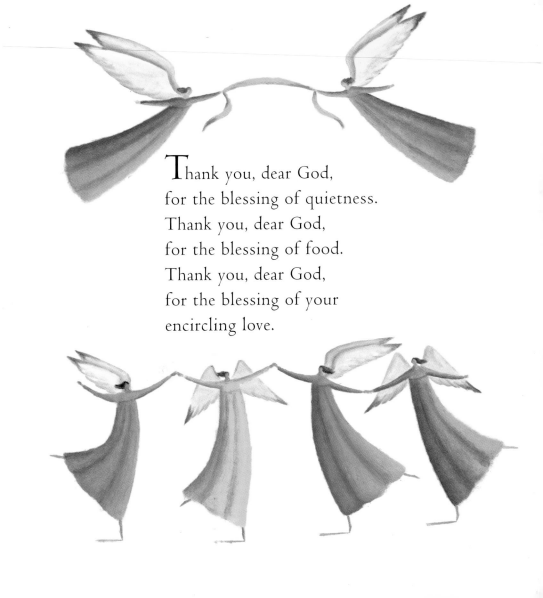

Thank you, dear God,
for the blessing of quietness.
Thank you, dear God,
for the blessing of food.
Thank you, dear God,
for the blessing of your
encircling love.

Our family

Thank you, dear God,
that we can meet together
and eat together
and pray together
and stay together.

We are hungry,
We have food,
We are family,
God is good.

Friends around the table

For our food and those who prepare it;
For health and friends to share it,
We thank you, Lord.

Anonymous

Let us take a moment
To thank God for our food,
For friends around the table
And everything that's good.

Out of doors

We thank thee, Lord, for happy hearts,
For rain and sunny weather,
We thank thee, Lord, for this our food,
And that we are together.

Emilie Fendall Johnson

Us and this: God bless.

A Quaker grace

Our daily bread

Heavenly Father,
Give us this day our daily bread.

From Luke 11:2–3

We remember the day that Jesus accepted a gift of five loaves and two fish. He looked up to heaven and thanked God for them. Then he broke them and gave them to his disciples to share with the crowd of people. They all ate and had enough.

From Luke 9:16–17

Hunger satisfied

We give thanks for our hunger,
We give thanks for our food,
We give thanks for enough of each
To do our bodies good.

For food in a world where many walk in hunger;
For faith in a world where many walk in fear;
For friends in a world where many walk alone,
We give you humble thanks, O Lord.

A Girl Guide world hunger grace

Harvest thanksgiving

Bless the earth
and bless the seed:
We have all the food we need.

Bless the sunshine,
bless the air:
We have food enough to share.

Harvest time is gold and red:
Thank God for our daily bread.

All good gifts around us
Are sent from heaven above,
Then thank the Lord, O thank the Lord,
For all his love.

Matthias Claudius (1740–1815),
translated by Jane Montgomery Campbell (1817–78)

Thank you everyone

God bless those who grew all this food.
  May they enjoy good food, too.
God bless those who helped harvest this food.
  May they enjoy good food, too.
God bless those who transported this food.
  May they enjoy good food, too.

God bless those who sold us this food.

    May they enjoy good food, too.

God bless those who prepared this food.

    May they enjoy good food, too.

God bless us as we eat this food.

    May we enjoy this good food and be thankful.

From around the world

Each time we eat,
may we remember God's love.

A Chinese grace

The bread is warm and fresh,
The water cool and clear.
Lord of all life, be with us,
Lord of all life, be near.

An African grace

Thank you for the rice that sustains my body:
most honorable food.

Thank you for the love that sustains my soul:
most honorable God.

A Japanese grace

From long ago

To God who gives our daily bread
A thankful song we raise,
And pray that he who sends us food
May fill our hearts with praise.

Thomas Tallis (c. 1505–85)

Bless me, O Lord, and let my food
strengthen me to serve thee, for
Jesus Christ's sake.

Isaac Watts (1674–1748)

Be present at our table, Lord,
Be here and everywhere adored;
Thy creatures bless and grant that we
May feast in paradise with thee.

John Cennick (1718–55)

After eating

Thank you, dear God, for the food I have eaten
and enjoyed. Thank you for the comfortable
feeling of being satisfied. I am grateful for
this and all your blessings.

Thank you for good food
that makes me strong:
strong to do good.